T0160941

Since 2013, every year on September 30th, we wear orange shirts to honour
Residential School survivors like Phyllis. We honour their experiences
and the experiences of their families. Orange Shirt Day is an opportunity
for First Nations, local governments, schools and communities
to all come together in the spirit of reconciliation and hope
for future generations of children.

It is a day to reaffirm that EVERY CHILD MATTERS.
Phyllis is so thankful that children are learning about First Nation's history.
It is something she learned little about when she was at school.
It is important that we know our (and each other's) histories.
She is overjoyed that you are taking part and learning the
true history of the first peoples of Canada.

For more information on Orange Shirt Day, visit www.orangeshirtday.org.
For some families, the topic of residential schools is very sensitive and difficult.
If you need crisis support, please contact the
Indian Residential Schools Resolution Health Support Program
1-866-925-4419.

Editor: Allison Parker
Text and illustration copyright © Medicine Wheel Education 2019
Printed in PRC
ISBN: 978-1-9891222-4-2
For more information, visit www.orangeshirtbook.com OR www.medicinewheel.education.

Phyllis's Orange Shirt

Written by **Phyllis Webstad**
Illustrated by **Brock Nicol**

Phyllis's Orange Shirt is an adaptation of Phyllis Webstad's beautiful book **The Orange Shirt Story,** for a younger audience (ages 4-6). In order to make **The Orange Shirt Story** accessible and appropriate for this young age group, the story has been simplified, shortened and given a rhyming scheme. Additionally, some of the pictures have been replaced by gentler images. This book was made with Phyllis and has her enthusiastic approval, and we are excited to present it to you.

Little Phyllis lived with her Granny on the Dog Creek Reserve.

They would pick berries, garden and catch fish to preserve.

There were not many kids with whom Phyllis could play

because they went to residential school far, far away.

One day Granny took Phyllis to town.

It was exciting to see so many people around!

Granny took Phyllis to a shop full of clothes,
with hats for your head and socks for your toes.

Phyllis picked out a shirt that was so orange, shiny and bright,
and Granny bought it for her to wear with delight.

On the first day of residential school, Phyllis just couldn't wait.

She wore her orange shirt so that she would look great.

But when she arrived her mood started to change,

the place was so cold, unfriendly and strange.

Her bright orange shirt was taken away

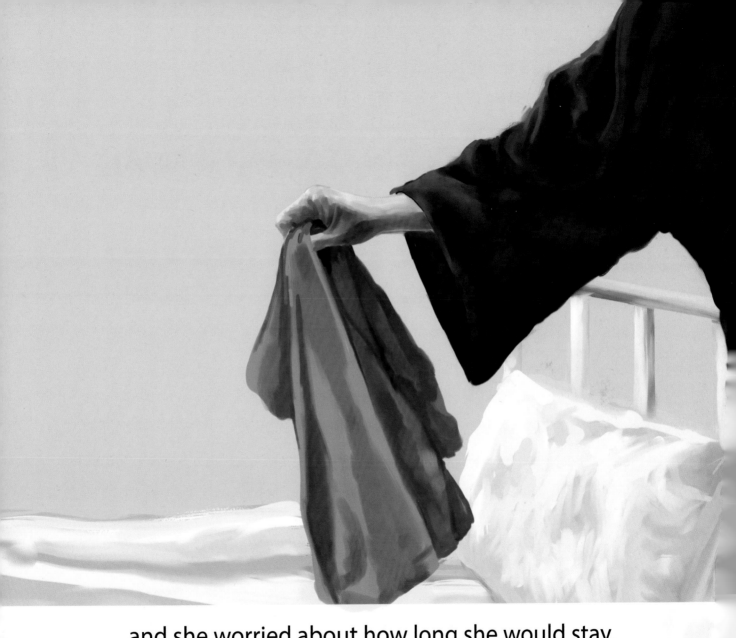

and she worried about how long she would stay.

At public school she was taught how to read and write neatly

by her teacher, who treated her so very sweetly.

Phyllis liked her teacher but missed her Granny so bad,

along with the garden and home that she had.

And then when finally summer arrived,

Phyllis returned to the home where she thrived.

We wear our orange shirts to remember
that every child matters, and not just in September!

We honour First Nations people and reflect
on how every child is special and deserves our respect.

September 30th-Orange Shirt Day:
Today the residential schools have closed for good.
Phyllis and her family learn about and celebrate their culture. Phyllis knows what it means
to be Northern Secwépemc, and is proud of who she is and who her people are.

Each year, on September 30th, many people, including Phyllis,
wear bright orange shirts to honour residential school survivors
and their families. Orange Shirt Day kicks off with talks about anti racism and bullying
at the beginning of the school year. Phyllis's true story is only one among many.
We must listen to these stories, and we must learn from our past. By doing so,
we can walk into the future without making the same mistakes again.
When we wear our orange shirts on Orange Shirt Day, we reaffirm that
every child matters- the children from every nation around the world,
the residential school survivors, and the First Nations children
who didn't come home.

About the Author:
Phyllis Webstad (nee Jack) is Northern Secwépemc (Shuswap) from the
Stswecem'c Xgat'tem First Nation (Canoe Creek Indian Band).
She comes from mixed Secwépemc and Irish/French heritage.
She was born in Dog Creek and lives in Williams Lake, BC.
Phyllis is married, has a son, a stepson, three grandsons and one
granddaughter.

Every year, Phyllis and her family camp by the Fraser River near Williams Lake.
The old and the young come together to catch and dry fish just like
their ancestors did. These are lessons that Phyllis learned as a child.
Now, she is proud to teach her grandchildren the ways of her people.
Phyllis is a third-generation residential school survivor.

BEYOND THE ORANGE SHIRT STORY

Phyllis Webstad

A collection of stories from family and friends of Phyllis Webstad before, during, and after their Residential School experiences.

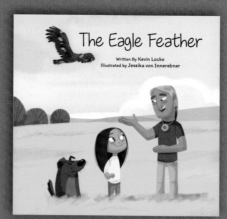
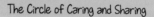

The Eagle Feather

Written By Kevin Locke
Illustrated by Jessika von Innerebner

Trudy's Healing Stone

Written by Trudy Spiller
Illustrated by Jessika von Innerebner

The Circle of Caring and Sharing

Written by Theresa "Corky" Larsen-Jonasson
Illustrated by Jessika von Innerebner

The Hoop Dancer's Teachings

Written by Teddy Anderson
Illustrated by Jessika von Innerebner

ORANGE SHIRT DAY
SEPTEMBER 30TH

Orange Shirt Society

Edited and Approved by
Phyllis Webstad & Joan Sorley

Every Child Matters

Gifts from Raven

Written by Kung Jaadee
Illustrated by Jessika von Innerebner

Phyllis's Orange Shirt

Written by Phyllis Webstad
Illustrated by Brock Nicol

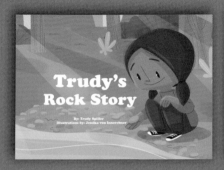

Trudy's Rock Story
By: Trudy Spiller
Illustrations by: Jessika von Innerebner

The Orange Shirt Story
Author: Phyllis Webstad
Illustrations: Brock Nicol

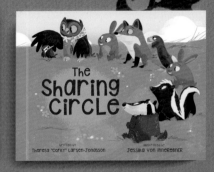

The Sharing Circle
Written by Theresa "Corky" Larsen-Jonasson
Illustrated by Jessika von Innerebner

Raven's Feast
by Kung Jaadee
Illustrated by Jessika von Innerebner

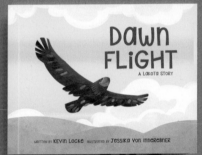

Dawn Flight
A Lakota Story
Written by Kevin Locke
Illustrated by Jessika von Innerebner

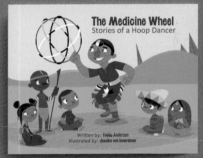

The Medicine Wheel
Stories of a Hoop Dancer
Written by: Teddy Anderson
Illustrated by: Jessika von Innerebner

This Is What I've Been Told
Mii Yi Gaa-Bi-Wiindmaagooyáng
Written & Illustrated by Juliana Armstrong

Meet Your Family
Gikenim Giniigi'Igoog
David Bouchard

We Learn from the Sun
David Bouchard
Paintings by Kristy Cameron

Visit our online store at:
www.medicinewheel.education

MEDICINE WHEEL
EDUCATION

www.medicinewheel.education

Online Courses Available:
www.classroom.medicinewheel.education

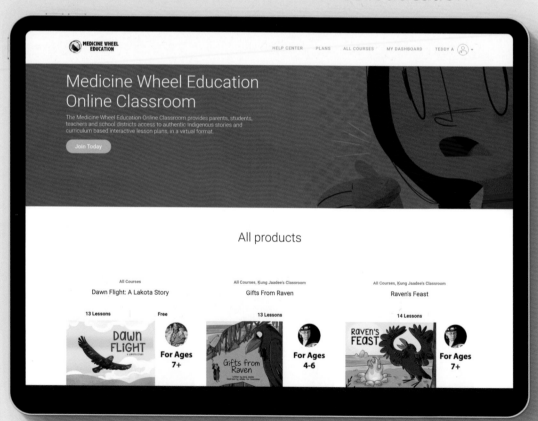

Online Classroom
By Medicine Wheel Education

Come in and join our online community where we gather together to learn through the gift of authentic Indigenous story-telling.

Learn More

www.medicinewheel.education/classroom

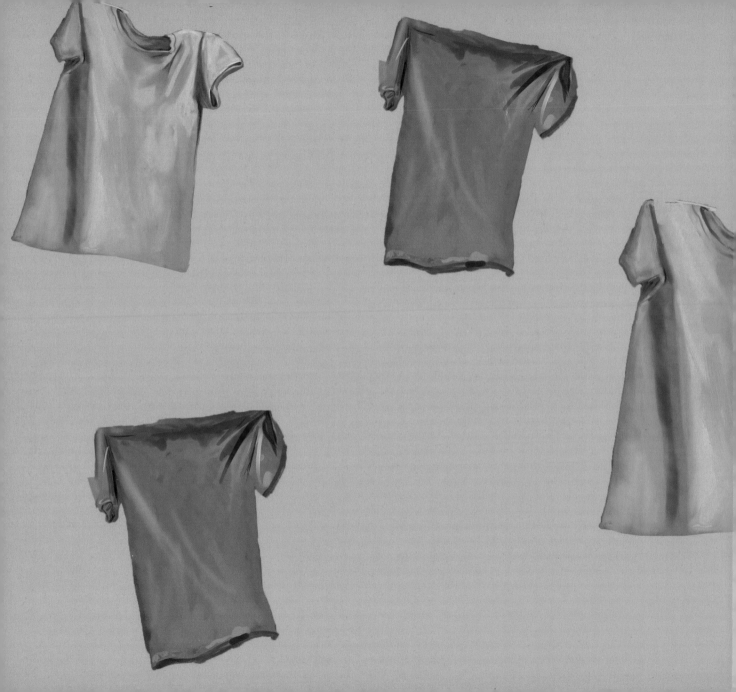